Copyright 2020 by

Alison Holmes

VINTAGE COLORING BOOKS

retro coloring books for adults

VINTAGE
WOMEN

grayscale coloring books for adults

Alison Holmes
VICTORIAN

Victorian Christmas Coloring Book

Old Time and Vintage
COLORING BOOKS

OLD FASHIONED CHRISTMAS COLORING BOOKS FOR ADULTS RELAXATION

Grayscale vintage coloring books for adults

Alison Holmes
VINTAGE COLORING BOOKS

The good **OLD TIME** *retro coloring books for adults*

Alison Holmes
VINTAGE COLORING BOOKS

A Funny
VINTAGE HORSE

coloring book & horse notebook with blank pages in one

Alison Holmes
VINTAGE COLORING BOOKS

retro coloring books for adults

VINTAGE WOMEN

grayscale coloring books for adults